VA Mortgages Declassified

Don't let the bank rip you off

Jason John Sharon
NMLS 1281448
Copyright 2019 Jason John Sharon
Updated for 2025

MISSION:

Educate and equip veterans to use VA backed mortgage loans properly and efficiently without getting ripped off.

What this book is and what it isn't:

I wanted to write a book that would educate veterans about the home-buying process but not be too technical. You are welcome, Marine. (hehe!)

I did not want it to be a commercial for me. It is not an advertisement or solicitation.

It truly is my experience as a loan officer, who is also a veteran, in my attempt at an "easy to comprehend and apply" format to prevent you from being screwed by the banks.

The 2 biggest veteran preferred banks (I won't name them because they have a lot more money to pay lawyers than I do) are NOT the best choice for you 95% of the time. Every once in a while I see situations where they are, but usually not.

Chapters

1 - The VA does not loan you money
2 - The biggest rip off: origination fees
3 - Mortgage approval basic training
4 - Credit score
5 - Debt to income - that's a crap load of math
6 - Down Payment and Eligibility - more than one loan
7 - Co-borrowers - this isn't your typical buddy system
8 - VA funding fees - this doesn't look right
9 - Appraisals - what's it worth to ya?
10 - Underwriting - automatic and manual
11 - Self employed/commission/bonuses - all income is not created equal
12 - Student loans
13 - Buying land and building
14 - Interest Rate Reduction Refinancing Loan (IRRRL)
15 - VA mortgage timelines - don't be your worst enemy
16 - VA Mortgage Assumptions - you know what ASSUME stands for
17 - Brokers vs lenders - MUST READ CHAPTER
18 - Discount Points - the daylight savings of mortgages
19 - Post closing solicitations - shred that crap
20 - How to pick a real estate agent
21 - Condominiums suck
22 - Interest rates and fees
23 - New Construction Builders - smoke and mirrors
24 - Learn how not to get screwed on a Loan Estimate
25 - Why a VA mortgage is better than a conventional mortgage
26 - How to find me - who am I?

Chapter 1: First, and probably most important:

The VA does NOT loan you money.

The government does not loan you money. Companies loan you the money.

The companies that have the word "veteran" in their name are not the VA. They are simply trying to establish immediate trust using a misleading name. I do not like that and do not condone that practice. I think it is similar to when you and I were overseas and see the slightly misspelled American brand names. Or the fake rolexes "bling bling for you my friend". I ask these companies, "if you have to make it seem like you are the VA, why?" I won't mention any to prevent legal slander issues. But we veterans need to think, why the mis-representation?

So where does the money come from? From investors.

So what does the VA do if they don't loan the money? The VA essentially issues an "insurance policy" on your loan. If you fail to pay your mortgage and the bank forecloses on you, the VA will pay up to 25% of the loan amount to the investor.

We will revisit that 25% number later.

Chapter 2 The biggest rip off: Origination fees.

The VA allows up to 1% origination fee. Allow: al·low -əˈlou/ verb give permission to do something.

Let's look at chapter 8 Paragraph 2.d of the VA guidelines:
In addition to the "itemized fees and charges," the lender may charge the veteran a flat charge not to exceed 1% of the loan amount.

Here is a confession, for the first 3 years of my career as a mortgage loan originator, I charged every single veteran (almost 100 veterans) that 1% funding fee. I was told by my employer what to do and how to do it. I did not know any better. So to all the veterans I screwed: I apologize.

I truly was following orders and trying to help. Since I left and started my own mortgage company, I have not charged that "allowable" fee.

So what exactly is this 1% flat fee? It is a rip off, that is what it is! It is extra profit the lender is making on you. It is complete bull crap, and you should not agree to it. You may see a processing or underwriting fee for less than $1000, that is ok.

To the lenders out there, I know how you make money. You make it by the spread on the rate and on selling the loan. You buy that money and then loan it to the veteran. Then you sell that mortgage to an investor for 4-5% of the loan amount. It costs you about 2-2.5% to pay the dozen or so employees that are responsible for the mortgage. Then you make an additional 1% when you sell the loan. Do we vet's think it is ok to pay and extra $2000-4000 to some lender that doesn't care about us and our sacrifices? Hell no we don't!

Check chapter 24 to learn how not to get screwed on a loan estimate.

Chapter 3 Mortgage approval basic training

The 3 C's of Mortgage Underwriting: Character, Capacity, and Collateral. If you have all these, you will be approved. If you are not approved, your loan officer sucks.

Character:
-Is your credit score high enough?
Usually 580. Higher is better for 2 reasons lower rate and less stipulations from the underwriter

-Do you have sufficient credit depth?
Generally, three lines of credit with all on time payments in last 12 months

Capacity:
-Do you make enough money to cover all your debts, including the new mortgage?
Debts divided by your gross monthly income is lower than 50%. I have seen many exceptions to this with compensating factors.

-Do you have a high probability of continuing to make that same income?
Two years of stable job history is the best. However, if you do not have that, do not worry.

Collateral:
-Is the house worth at least the amount you want to borrow?
The VA appraisal will determine this.

-Is the title of the home clear and warrantable?
Your title company will determine this.

Chapter 4 Credit Score

What is a credit score? It is a secret sauce calculation by the 3 main credit bureaus of their estimate of the likelihood that you will repay your debt.

There is no minimum credit score in the VA guidelines. None, nada, zilch.

However the lender may have a minimum score. Many lenders require your middle score to be at least a 620. If your score is below 640, generally you will need some compensating factors to strengthen your loan application.

Personally, I have closed VA mortgages down in the 560 range. Obviously the higher your score, the better interest rate you will get and the easier your loan process will be. The fastest way to increase your score is to pay down revolving debt. Once your credit card balances go above 10% of the limit, your score starts to drop. Above 50%, it really drops. Having a balance of 1-4% will help your score the most.

Do you have three lines of credit with at least 12-months good payment history? If not, many lenders can use alternate lines of credit: rent history, cell phone bills, car insurance, netflix subscriptions, etc.

But my score on this website says my score is higher… So it costs me (and every other mortgage company out there) to pull your credit. The credit bureaus are "for profit" companies. They are not giving your score away for free. So those "free" websites are using the free data to estimate your score. The "not free" sites are probably using a different scoring model than a mortgage credit pull requires.

I like to say that online credit scores are 20 points optimistic.

Chapter 5 Debt to income - too much math

(DTI) ratio is your total monthly debt payments divided by your gross monthly income.

Let's assume you are an E-6 over 8 years (base pay of about $3500/mo), with housing allowance of $1500/mo, and subsistence allowance of $365/mo. Your total monthly income is $5365/mo

VA guidelines do not have DTI limits, but as a thumb rule, I limit my preapprovals to 50%. I've closed loans up to 75%.
(Hi Elizabeth!)

So if you make $5365/month, I would not issue a prequal letter with a mortgage payment that exceeds $2682 minus your other monthly debts. Those other debts include car payments, student loans (these are special and we will discuss more later), credit card minimum payments, boat loans, timeshares, your fiance's engagement ring, military star card, etc.

let's show a real life example:
car loan $400/mo, your 3 credit cards total $182/mo minimum payment, and you have a ring payment of $100/mo. Your total debt payment per month is $400 + $182 + $100 = $682.
$2682 - $682 = $2000/mo available for a mortgage payment.

Here is a very handy thumb rule: your mortgage payment will be about $7/month for every $1000 in purchase price, including taxes and insurance. That works for most of America, excluding places that have high property taxes and flood zones.

A $100,000 house will have a payment of about $700/month
A $200,000 house will have a payment of about $1400/month
A $300,000 house will have a payment of about $2100/month

A $400,000 house will have a payment of about $2800/month

I just divide the $ available for your mortgage by $7 to arrive at the maximum purchase price you are approved for.

$2000 / $7 = $285,714 purchase price.

Now I am not saying go run and look for that much house. I am simply showing you how the scratch pad math works on preapprovals. You should have a written budget in complete agreement with your spouse, otherwise you will not make smart financial decisions.

Chapter 6 More than one VA mortgage - Eligibility vs Down payment

I see and hear so much misinformation on this topic.

You can have more than one VA mortgage at a time AND You can use your VA eligibility more than once.

I believe this myth comes from misunderstanding that VA mortgage can only be utilized to purchase a primary residence. If you are PCSing from TX to SC you can rent out that home in TX and get a 2nd VA mortgage in SC. Your loan amount may be limited.

In 2019, the Blue Water Navy Act changed VA eligibility a lot. Now there is no limit to your VA eligibility if you do not have an encumbrance on your COE. What does that mean? If you do not have another VA mortgage or a short sale or foreclosure, you can get a VA loan for as high as you can afford. Yes, you can buy a $2,000,000 home with no down payment and no PMI. Crazy huh?

Now, let's talk about eligibility scenarios where you have an encumbrance on your COE. Remember that 25% that we discussed earlier? The VA insures 25% of your mortgage, up to $806,500 total loan amount (in 2025). That total loan amount is higher in "high cost" counties such as NYC, San Fran, Wash DC, etc, but it is the true number for most of America.

Let's assume your original loan amount for your home that you are retaining was $300,000, your eligibility will be limited to $806,500 - $300,000 = $506,500. You may be approved for more, or less, depending on your DTI.

But I want and can afford to buy a more expensive house. Great!

You will have a down payment equal to 25% of the purchase price above your eligibility limit. So if you have remaining eligibility of $425,000, and you want to buy a home for $525,000, you will have a downpayment of $25,000.

$525,000 - $425,000 = $100,000 then $100,000 * 25% = $25,000

One side note here: VA set up eligibility completely bass-ackwards: You have basic entitlement up to $144,000, then bonus entitlement up to $806,500. So if you have an existing encumbrance on your COA (even if less than $144,000), like in the previous example, your new loan MUST be greater than $144,000.

Chapter 7 Co-borrowers - not your typical "buddy system"

You can use your VA loan with a non-spouse co-borrower.

They will be required to have a down payment of 12.5% of the purchase price. The problem you will run into, most investors will not fund this type of loan since 12.5% is a lot of risk.

This scenario requires the VA regional loan center to approve your loan prior to closing. So once the lender fully approves your loan, they have to send the entire package to the appropriate VA regional office. This can add a week or two to your closing timeline.

Common questions I get:

Should I put my spouse on the loan?

That depends on his/her credit and DTI. If you can qualify on your own, usually it is smarter to keep it that way. If you add a spouse with a lower credit score, that will make your interest rate increase. If you add a spouse with a higher DTI that you, that will make it a more difficult approval process.

Can my veteran brother co sign for me because I do not make much money?
A non-occupying veteran can co sign. Though you can not use their VA loan eligibility. The income of the non-occupying co signer can not make up for a lack of income for the veteran.

Chapter 8 VA Funding Fee - this doesn't look right

Your loan amount is going to look weird on your disclosures. ⇐ remember this

The VA is going to charge you a funding fee, unless you have a disability rating. This fee is normally rolled into the loan, giving you a higher loan amount than you expect.

There are a myriad of different funding fees, most common is 2.15%. The exact % depends on your type of service and number of VA mortgages you have had.

So your $300,000 purchase will probably have a loan amount of $306,450.

On your 2nd and subsequent VA loans, your funding fee will probably be 3.3%. If you have a downpayment of at least 5%, your funding fee will be greatly reduced.

If you are using the special refinance program called Interest Rate Reduction Refinancing Loan (IRRRL), your funding fee will probably be 0.5%.

Chapter 9 Appraisal

Your VA appraisal is not a home inspection. <-- important to remember

The appraiser is required to verify the property meets certain minimum property conditions. However, this does not replace a quality home inspection by a licensed inspector. You should employ a licensed home inspector to perform a thorough inspection. Your real estate agent will probably know a handful of inspectors to recommend. I highly suggest you attend the inspection. Inspections average about $600. Be prepared that the inspection report could exceed 20 pages. That does not mean the home is in poor condition, it means the inspector was thorough. Your real estate agent should help with the proper perspective on the inspection results.

The VA appraiser is not employed by the VA. He/she is probably a small business owner who was approved by the VA to perform appraisals. The cost varies state to state, in SC in 2025 the VA appraisals cost about $600 except for the high demand counties. The VA has a page on their site with current appraisal costs and turn times. The national average is about $650.

The home must be structurally sound, safe, and sanitary. Chapter 12 of the guidelines contains 24 pages detailing the minimum property conditions (commonly referred to as MPCs).

To summarize: No broken windows, no busted drywall, no active roof leaks, no open ended pipes, no exposed electrical, no missing roof shingles, all installed appliances in reasonable working order, and complete floor covering. Got it Chair Force? hehe!

Do not think you are going to buy a foreclosure, short sale, handyman special, or a fix-er-upper with a VA loan. Why?

Because those types of sellers will usually not pay for repairs, so you are not going to meet one of the 3 C's from the previous chapter. Basically, the appraisal will be "subject to repairs". If those repairs are not completed, you can not close that loan. There are VA renovation loans and escrow hold back options for these scenarios. They are not common and generally more expensive loan options. But if you love the house...

BIG MYTH: VA appraisals are harder than other types of appraisals. It is very unfortunate that many people believe this. If you examine the appraisal processes for VA loans and others, VA appraisals actually have 2 formal options to "appeal" a low value, whereas other loan types have no formal options. These are called the Tidewater process and the Reconsideration of Value (ROV). I have a great video on my youtube channel about this.

The ROV, in a nutshell, is where you, the veteran, appeal directly to the VA regional loan center about the assigned value. I have done this dozens of times and been successful more often than not. Basically you write a letter to the VA stating what you think it is worth and the basis for that. You also include up to 3 comparable properties that support your numbers. If you are compelling, the VA will issue a higher value appraisal. Watch my youtube video on it and ask me questions if you need help.

Chapter 10 Underwriting

There are 2 parts to the underwriting of a loan, a computer system and then a person who reviews your documentation.

All loans are submitted to an Automated Underwriting System (AUS). There are two used for VA loans: Fannie Mae's Desktop Underwriter and Freddie Mac's Loan Prospector. Really, these are just computer servers where your loan application and credit report are submitted electronically for approval. The servers perform a detailed calculation based on an algorithm comparing your credit history, your employment history, your income, your debts, your loan to value, and your assets all against predesigned risk factors to basically give a "thumbs up" or "thumbs down" for your scenario. If you get a "thumbs up", the actual underwriter performs a very basic easy review of your documents. They are looking for proof of what was reported in your loan application. However, if you get a "thumbs down", the person will need to make a judgment call about your creditworthiness. Typically, you will receive a favorable approval if you have 2 or more compensating factors in your file.

Common compensating factors include:
-low DTI
-conservative use of credit
-greater than 2 years employment history
-additional income not used in the income calculation
-housing expense increasing by less than 5%
-more than 120% residual income calculation
-greater than 2 mortgage payments saved in your savings account

Chapter 11 Self-employed/ commission/bonuses

If you are paid in any manner besides a steady salary or steady hourly rate, you will need at least 2 years of that pay to satisfy the VA's requirement that it has a high probability that you will continue to earn that compensation.

So if you started your own business last year, you will need to wait. The VA requires lenders to use the average profit (not gross) income for the last 2 years to prove stability for these situations.

Did you get a bonus last year but not the year before? Nope, can't use it

Are you paid with a small base salary plus commission? If you have less than 2 years history of that commission, you can only use the base salary.

Are you paid with tips in the food and beverage industry? If you didn't report those tips for a full 2 years, you can not use them.

Did you become a 1099 contractor in the last 2 years? No joy on any of that income. If more than 2 years, you can only use what you claimed for profit for the last 2 years from your Schedule C on your tax returns.

Did you start your own company more than 2 years ago? If so, you will need to provide your company tax returns so your loan officer can calculate income.

Chapter 12 Student Loans

VA is the most lenient loan program when it comes to student loans.

If your student loans are deferred more than 12 months after closing, they can be ignored. Yup, like they are not there. You can call the student loan servicer to get the deferment extended to meet this requirement.

If they are not deferred for more than 12 months (yes, even if deferred for 11 months), the underwriter will need to include a payment in your DTI calculation. Currently, the calculation is five percent of the balance, divided by 12.

Example: $30,000 in deferred student loans

$30,000 * 5% = $1500

$1500 / 12 = $125/mo added into your DTI calculation

Chapter 13 Buying land and building your home

You will have an amazingly difficult time with this.

While the VA does allow you to buy land and build, I only know three lenders that will fund this loan. With them, you can purchase a lot, pick a builder, close on the loan (30 year fixed), then the builder can build the house. The interest rate is a good bit higher than a standard VA loan. Also, the builder has costs associated with the loans, which will be passed onto you via the home price.

The VA prohibits veterans, like you and me, from paying the interest on the loan during the build process. Someone has to pay for it. Typically, the builder pays that interest and charges it back to you as a "builder fee". This will be tens of thousands of dollars.

Why is the rate a lot higher than normal? Well, the loan is not securitized until you move in. That means that the interest rate that the lender sells the loan at can be different than what they lent you. They would have to buy down that rate, which is a HUGE risk for them. Therefore they sell you a higher interest rate to mitigate that risk. It's not big deal, you can refi 210 days after you make your first payment, into a normal VA rate loan.

The builder has to be VA approved and has to be underwritten as well. This is where I see these loans go sideways. Builders don't like to participate in this process, because it is complex. It is not attractive to many investors.

Chapter 14 Interest Rate Reduction Refinancing Loan (IRRRL)

The VA created a streamlined loan for veterans like you and I that make refinancing amazingly easy. I have closed hundreds of these loans.

This loan product does not require income documentation, asset documentation, or an appraisal. Lenders can use a mortgage only credit report. Basically I tell my clients to send me your DL, your most recent mortgage statement and your original note to get started. Rarely do you need more than just those items.

Beware, there are lenders out there that churn VA IRRRL's, which is bad for us veterans. This was such a bad problem that new laws were created which require at least 210 days between the first payment on the loan you are paying off and the closing date of the new loan. Also, you must see at least a 0.5% drop in your interest rate, and the money you save over the 1st 36 months of the new loan must be greater than the fees in the refinance. This is called the recoup test.

Many people want to use an IRRRL to reduce the years in the term of the loan. Unfortunately, the VA made a rule to protect us that also had an unintended negative effect. That recoup test must pass or the loan can not close. Let's say you want to drop from a 30 year loan to a 15 year loan. Your payment WILL increase. Since you are not saving money per month, the recoup test will fail and the loan can not close. In my experience, you will probably be able to refi into a 25 year loan, but any shorter than that usually fails the recoup test.

Chapter 15 VA mortgage timelines

There are some timelines you need to be aware of so you do not make your loan application more difficult than it already is.

From the time you have a complete application, the lender is required to send you your initial disclosures within 3 business days. How they make sure they stay in compliance is by having you e-sign those. If you do not e-sign them in time, you will need to wet sign them or they may have to resend them. This will delay your loan.

Your appraisal can not be ordered until you sign your intent to proceed. That is usually in your initial disclosure package. Different regions allow different time frames for the appraisal. A single data point, at the time of this publishing, SC affords the appraiser 9 business days for completion.

When you have a change of circumstance, the lender must send you a new loan estimate. There must be at least 24 hours between a loan estimate and your closing disclosure. So if you are changing your mind on something late in the loan, it will cause a delay.

Your closing disclosure must be signed at least 4 days prior to closing. Small things can and will probably change, but the initial closing disclosure starts a 4 day clock.

For a refi, you have a 3 day right of rescission. Therefore any delays you cause may result in you exceeding your lock period which will cost you money.

Chapter 16 VA mortgage assumption

2 points: assuming a mortgage and allowing someone to assume your mortgage. Both scenarios take about 90 days, as current in 2025 data.

A - You can assume another veteran's mortgage. It may be smart based on the note rate compared to the current market. You will perform the assumption through the seller's current mortgage company. You will need to qualify through them. Additionally, you will need to figure out how you are going to pay for the difference between the mortgage balance and the sales price. You could get a 2nd mortgage for that, but the mortgage details and terms will need to be approved by the current mortgage company. After closing, you should contact the VA to transfer the eligibility from the seller's COE to your COE, though this is not required.

B - You can allow another person (this does NOT have to be a veteran) to assume your current mortgage in a sales transaction. I strongly suggest against this plan. While that mortgage is outstanding, it will reduce the amount of remaining eligibility you have available to buy your next home. Even worse, if they are not the most upstanding individuals and have a foreclosure, this will cloud your certificate of eligibility until you pay off their debt. The buyer must qualify through your current mortgage company for this plus come up with the difference in money. Check with your mortgage company about their turnaround times. This may hinder your next purchase transaction time frame and force you to rent.

My opinion? Just don't do it.

Chapter 17 Brokers vs lenders

Online lender, depository institution (bank or credit union), correspondent lender (a retail location that only originates mortgages), or a mortgage broker? Only a broker represents YOUR best interests. All other loan originators are w-2 employees hired for their company's bottom line.

Why not an online lender? They have no customer service motivation. That loan officer is all about getting you committed to him. True stat: they compete on 11% of all loan applications but close less than 5%.

Why not depository? They have little skill and they are limited to their own loan products. Do you want fries with that mortgage?

Why not retail lending? The most expensive and again, limited to only the loan products their one lending source has to offer. Usually better customer service and slightly more loan products.

What are brokers bound to? I am **REQUIRED** by the SC Department of Consumer Affairs to work in your best interest **EXACTLY** like your realtor. Retail LO's are not bound by that regulatory requirement. They are simply w-2 employees with managers to please. Of course, there is a level of ethics to uphold, but don't forget they work for the bottom line.

How does a broker save me money? When I represent your loan, lenders compete to earn your business. They know I have over a dozen places to submit your loan. Lender comparison and loan analysis drive competition in the wholesale market place.

The maximum a broker can earn on a loan is 275 basis points (2.75% of the loan amount). The average retail earned 379 basis points in 2017 (Mortgage Banker Association report April 16, 2018). That is 37% more expensive than a broker.

How does a broker save the lender money? The origination and processing tasks are completed by the broker, the underwriting and funding tasks are completed by the lender. The broker just cut the lender's compliance and staffing bill in half! Therefore, wholesale rates are lower than retail. I see that when I check the wholesale rate sheets compared to the retail sheet.

Can't you steer me to the loan that pays you the most and I won't even know? Nope, federal law requires a broker to set lender paid compensation exactly the same with each lender source.

Chapter 18 Discount points / buying down your rate

Discount points are prepaid interest charges.

Basically you are paying some additional interest now so that you pay less interest later. So the decision you need to make, with your loan officer's guidance, is how much is it going to save me during the time I will own the home versus how much it is going to cost me. I look at it like daylight savings. You aren't saving anything. Just moving daylight around.

My opinion: the first bit to buy down your rate is usually worth it. But the 2nd 1/8% buy down is usually not. If it costs you $1000 to buy down your rate 1/8% which saves you $20/mo, it will take you 50 months to realize that savings. If you are probably going to sell the home in 3 years, you just threw away money.

Chapter 19 Post-closing solicitations

When you close on your mortgage, the fact that you have a VA mortgage will become public record.

There are companies that mine public data to solicit their products to you.

I will happily say that most of those products are crap. You will get solicitations to refi (already discussed loan churn companies), bi-weekly payments, mortgage life insurance, dismemberment insurance, selling you a copy of your deed, and all kinds of other stuff.

Chances are the lender did not sell your information. If you are unsure of anything you get in the mail, ask your mortgage officer or your real estate agent. If it sounds too good to be true, it is.

My opinion: If you can't explain it so that your grandma understands it, then you don't understand it. So don't buy it or invest in it.

Chapter 20 How to pick a real estate agent

The best way to pick any service provider is to get a referral from someone. Not just anyone providing the referral, but a referral source who knows that service industry and knows many options for that service.

Who better than a local mortgage professional? No one!

Notice I said "local". There are companies out there that will pay you to use their referral partner. Um, that sounds like steering. You and I both know there is no such thing as free money.

Why local? Because an agent that is really good in one zip code may not be really good 2 counties over. Or they may be really good as a listing agent, but not have the negotiating experience as a buyer's agent. Or they may be really good at new construction, but not condos. Follow my point now?

You want an agent that knows VA loans well, and will fight for you.

Find a local mortgage broker (refer to that earlier chapter), then ask them who they would recommend for your unique situation.

Chapter 21 Condominiums suck

Condo's suck.

The developer chose to create a different legal entity for the properties than what you and I are probably used to. The legal connection between units is stronger and tighter than a town home or a homeowners association. A legal battle for your neighbor can and will probably affect you in your condo. Not so much for your townhouse neighbor or your single family detached neighbor.

Now, you are dead set on this condo, what next? The VA only will insure loans for condos if they are on the VA approved condo list. That list is small, and it is difficult to navigate. Make sure your loan officer is really experienced in this arena. I have closed VA condo loans that other mortgage loan officers declined for not being on the list. Why? Because the list is fricken hard to understand. You know the government…

But the online website says it is a town home… I do not believe any listing agents. They selected "town home" because their seller stated it is a town home. However, the seller is probably wrong and doesn't realize it. You (or your real estate agent) MUST go to the county website to verify the legal entity of that home.

The VA does have a process to get a condo association approved. The HOA will have to complete a lot of paperwork and submit a lot of documents.

Chapter 22 - Interest Rates

What is an interest rate? Like really?

Interest is the cost to borrow money. The most simple way to explain it: it is the supply and demand of the US dollar. How many dollars are out there to be borrowed and how many people want to borrow them? Think of the pretty girls at the high school dance: not many of them there but most of the guys want to dance with them. Note, I was not one of the guys that got to dance with them.

So where do these dollars come from? From investors that want a safe steady return on their money. The safest return is the US 10 year treasury bill, also called a T-bill. So the biggest competitor for investment dollars is the T-bill. Therefore mortgage rates must be higher than the T-bill rate. So what affects the T-bill? The US economy affects it. If the economy is doing well, the government must raise the T-bill rate to keep investor cash flow into the T-bill. If the T-bill rises, mortgage rates must rise as well to keep investors putting money into the mortgage market.

Of course, this is an over-simplification. Hopefully it makes a little sense to you. I tried to make it so the Army could understand… hehe!

Chapter 23 - New construction preferred lenders - smoke and mirrors

Ok, this topic really pissed me off. You want a new home, yes, everyone does. You drive by a new neighborhood and stop in the sales office. The onsite agent is professional and helpful. A few days later you decide to build that one floor plan on one of those 2 lots you really like. You set the appointment, spend 2 hours on the paperwork, and sign a ton of stuff. They tell you they will give you $6000 towards closing costs if you use their preferred lender. You ask "why?" Oh, because they know how to properly qualify people and they know our systems and how we work. It will be soooo much easier for you, if you use them. It means so much to us, that we will give you money to use them. Hold up, why does that even make sense? You, the builder, are going to give me money to use some other companies? Wait, maybe the preferred lender is going to give you money to use them. What? You mean they are going to lose money for me? Are you catching my drift here?

You and I both know there is no such thing as free money. In this scenario, one of two things are happening: the builder is artificially inflating the price of the home or the lender is artificially raising your interest rate, along with up front fees, to give you a "credit." How do I know? Because I was that guy back in 2016-2017.

-What you really need to know with a neighborhood builder:
A - Their agent does not represent you. You NEED to have your own real estate agent. It is free for you and can save you from a bad mistake.
B - Their preferred lender does not consider you their #1 client. The builder is their client, not you. They MUST keep the builder happy so that the builder will continue to refer borrowers to them. Think about that.
C - The builder probably has partial ownership of the lender or receives financial compensation from your loan.

Chapter 24 - How not to get screwed on a Loan Estimate (LE)

The biggest sham I see is a lender sending a borrower a fee sheet. Most borrowers will look at it, think, "ok, seems reasonable" then proceed forward with the loan. A fee sheet is COMPLETE CRAP! If you want to compare apples to apples, you have to compare Loan Estimates. If the loan estimates are too far off to make sense, ask one of the loan officers to make an adjustment to match either the origination fees section or the rate of the other lender. That way you can really compare. If that still doesn't help, find my email later in this book and send me both of them. I'll help you out.

Here is what is important on the LE: rate, fees, and "is it locked?"

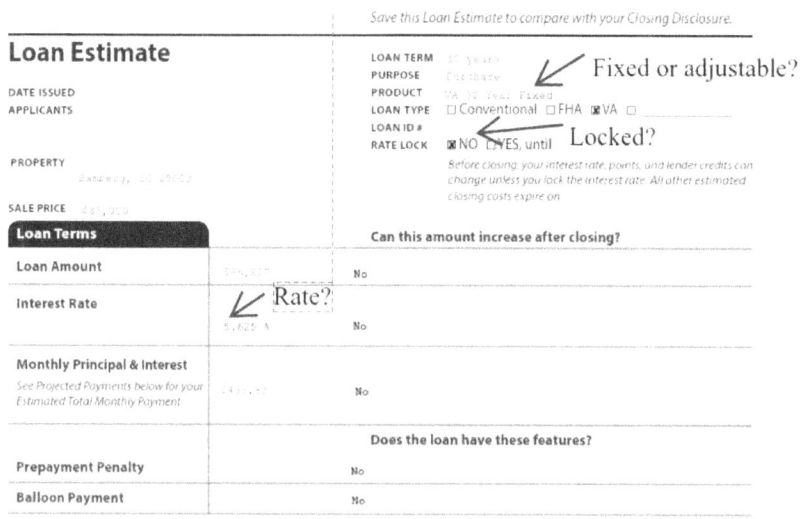

You also want to check for excessive fees here in section A and section B.

Closing Cost Details

Loan Costs

A. Origination Charges	$112
% of Loan Amount (Points)	

A small discount fee here is ok. As is an appraisal fee.

B. Services You Cannot Shop For	$1,898

The funding fee and a few small fees are ok here.

Other Costs

E. Taxes and Other Government Fees	$50
Recording Fees and Other Taxes	
Transfer Taxes	

F. Prepaids	$595
Homeowner's Insurance Premium (months)	
Mortgage Insurance Premium (months)	
Prepaid Interest (per day for days)	
Property Taxes (months)	

G. Initial Escrow Payment at Closing	$180
Homeowner's Insurance per month for mo.	
Mortgage Insurance per month for mo.	
Property Taxes per month for mo.	

H. Other	$200

Chapter 25 - Why a VA loan is superior to a conventional loan.

This should be required reading for real estate agents.

A VA loan is far superior for several reasons:

1-VA loans are 4% more likely to close per the Mortgage Bankers Association report in 2022.

2-VA loans are the only ones with a formal procedure to fight a low appraisal. There is the Tidewater process before the appraiser even issues a value. Then if the value still comes in low, the veteran may appeal directly to the VA for a Reconsideration of Value (ROV). I actually have a lot of luck on ROVs. Not so much on Tidewater. Also, VA appraisals have a set timeline that the appraiser must turn in the report. The same appraiser doing a VA appraisal and a conventional appraisal will make more money on the VA appraisal.

3-VA loans have fewer underwriters. Most people never think of this part. A conventional loan will also have an additional underwriter for the private mortgage insurance. That is an additional risk.

4-Since VA loans have no downpayment, there is more money available to use if the appraised value comes in low.

5-VA has an approved list for condos. So if you are doing a VA loan on a condo, you do not need to worry about the association being approved. Conventional loans have no such approved list. Each conventional loan must have a condo questionnaire completed by the home owners association. That is an additional costs for the borrower (reducing available funds). The questionnaire then must be reviewed by the underwriter. I have seen MANY associations not get approved for conventional loans.

6-VA loans have an average down payment of 12%. So it is not good to assume that the veteran is in a weak financial position.

7-VA guidelines are much more liberal than conventional underwriting guidelines. The underwriter is supposed to figure out how to make it work for the veteran. Conventional loans have no such direction. Actually, conventional loans are quite the opposite.
From the VA guidelines:

> Lenders are encouraged to make VA loans to all qualified Veterans who apply. VA's underwriting standards are intended to provide guidelines for underwriters. Decisions must be based on sound application of the standards, and underwriters are expected to use good judgment and flexibility in applying underwriting guidelines. Not all possible circumstances are addressed therefore, underwriters must apply reasonable judgment and flexibility in administering this important Veterans' benefit.

Chapter 26 - How to find me

This is not a solicitation for a loan.

This book was designed to educate you so you do not make bad decisions that cost you thousands of dollars. I am currently licensed in SC, NC, VA, WV, GA, FL, and AL.

If you have questions, feel free to email me Jason@homeloansinc.com or call me 843.LOW.RATE

About me:
I enlisted in the Navy in 1993, my senior year. Boot camp in Orlando from Aug - Oct (fricken hot!) Then four month A-school to be an electrician, promoted to E-4, (AIT for you Army types) and six month Nuclear Power School (physics and stuff). Did a small 3 month cushy instructor stint between those 2 schools. Got in a boat load of trouble in that 2nd school for not ratting on someone. Then transferred to Charleston, SC for my 3rd school: on the job training Nuclear Prototype. Promoted to E-5 in that school and was the 1st to qualify in my class, it was a self-paced school. Selected to teach that 3rd school for 2 years before I was sent to sea duty: USS Nimitz (CVN-68). Served on her for a few years, promoted to E-6. Qualified everything possible for myself. Then transferred back to Charleston Prototype to teach. Someone really liked me and allowed me to qualify as Engineering Officer of the Watch (normally only for officers, not lowly E-6's). This set me up to make Chief (E-7) in 2001. Then I was hand selected to be a real jerk as Naval Reactors. Basically an inspector. Did that for several years, and was commissioned in 2002. In 2003, I was transferred to USS ENTERPRISE as Radiological Controls Officer. That is where most of my grey hair came from. Spent a little time cross training on USS ANZIO (CG-68), got promoted to O-2E there. Transferred back to Charleston Prototype as an inspector again in 2005. Did a lot of stuff there, made O-3E. In 2011, I was transferred to Newport News Shipyard as an

inspector. Selected for O-4 Lieutenant Commander CY 2013, but declined the promotion because I was a geo-bachelor and did not want to spend one minute more away from my kids than I had to. Retired in Sep 2013 after 20 years and one month serving the finest country in the world. That last month felt longer than the first 20 years!

Disclaimer: I do not work for the VA and the VA did not review or approve this book. No lenders reviewed or approved this book. I wrote it from my years of experience closing over a thousand loans and reviewing thousands of applications.

www.ingramcontent.com/pod-product-compliance
Lightning Source LLC
Chambersburg PA
CBHW071200220526
45468CB00003B/1092